W. T. Cox

Out of the Depths

A PersonalNarrative of My Fall Under the Power of Strong Drink and My Complete

Reformation

W. T. Cox

Out of the Depths
A PersonalNarrative of My Fall Under the Power of Strong Drink and My Complete Reformation

ISBN/EAN: 9783743370999

Manufactured in Europe, USA, Canada, Australia, Japa

Cover: Foto ©Lupo / pixelio.de

Manufactured and distributed by brebook publishing software (www.brebook.com)

W. T. Cox

Out of the Depths

The Temperance Book for the Times.

OUT OF THE DEPTHS;

A

PERSONAL NARRATIVE

OF

My Fall Under the Power of Strong Drink

AND MY

COMPLETE REFORMATION.

BY W. T. COX.

"Out of the Depths have I cried unto Thee, O Lord."—Psa. cxxx. 1.

SYCAMORE, ILL.
BAKER & ARNOLD.
1876.

Pointed, Truthful, Heart-stirring.

Copyright applied for.

TO THE DEAR WIFE,

WHO STOOD

LOVINGLY BY MY SIDE

IN THE DARKEST HOUR

THAT CAN EVER

COME TO A HUMAN BEING,

THIS LITTLE VOLUME IS

AFFECTIONATELY INSCRIBED

BY THE AUTHOR.

Printed at the office of THE FREE METHODIST, Sycamore, Ill.

INTRODUCTION.

All over this land are to be found persons enslaved by strong drink, who long for deliverance, and yet fail to find any way out of their trouble. Many of these are men who once occupied places of trust and emolument. They were blessed with talents by the exercise of which they hoped to raise themselves to a high place in the estimation of their fellows, and be of much service to the world. While they maintained their integrity all was well. The world opened up grandly before them and it seemed that the bright visions of youth were about to be realized in the tangible realities of a noble manhood. They secured enough of material wealth to surround themselves and those dear to them with the comforts of life; and as they stored their minds with useful knowledge and engaged in the social pleasures surrounding them, it seemed as though life comprised very little but what was bright and joyous. But a change came. The very "large-heartedness," "whole-souledness" which rendered them the charm of their circle hastened their downfall. They learned the use of stimulants—learned to "tarry long at the wine," to dally with the Siren who comes at first with a goblet of nectar twined with flowers and accompanied by laughter and song; but who appears at last as a savage Fury, holding to bloated lips a chalice full of vipers of hell. It is the old sad, sad story, involving wreck of character, family-ruin, want, famine, sin—oh God! how much of sin!—and now they are cast out of society, and if something is not done for them quickly, they have nothing to hope for but the most miserable of all deaths—and the drunkard's awful hell.

Oh! my brethren in suffering! my heart bleeds while I think of the agony and shame and remorse that wrings your souls. Too well do I know what it is when the links of the "Devil's Chain" sink through the quivering flesh to the very bone; when the heart throbs with anguish; when the nerves start with agony, and the brain is on fire, for I have suffered it all. And it is for your sake, poor suffering ones that I stifle the pain it causes me to write some of the pages which follow.

This unpretentious little volume is no carefully prepared treatise on the general subject of Temperance. I need not point out the poisonous nature of alcohol, or the terrible evils, financial and social, it inflicts upon society and upon individuals; how it despoils manhood of its glory; snatches the bread out of the mouths of the poor little children; plucks hope out of the breast of the trembling wife, and fills the souls of its victims with the tortures of the lost. I feel no call to chide, and if I did, I am aware those I wish to reach know all about these things. But I *do feel* that, by the blessing of God, I can point out clearly how they may escape from all their troubles and get back to manhood, to friends, and to society—*saved men and women!*

Christian men and women! breathe an earnest prayer on these pages and send them into every poor, vile place in the land with the news that there is power in Jesus Christ to raise up the worst drunkard and make a *man* of him. I know it, for I have traveled over the whole ground, and having waited for four years and upwards before sending out this public statement, I am satisfied that the change wrought in me is permanent.

In a simple narrative form I present pages from my heart-experiences which will, I trust, prove a warning to the young, an inducement to the middle aged moderate drinker to stop and think, but above all to convey to the befogged mind of the drunkard the blessed idea that there is hope for him yet.

To show how a young man first becomes entangled in the meshes of this destroyer I have deemed it necessary to carry my life-story from an early period until the hour when I became a free man. Let the reader remember one thing: this is no isolated case. Hundreds have been saved by the same means, and, thank God, the same personal experience is for all who will accept of it.

Oh! may the Being who has done so much for me, take these words, warm from my heart, and carry them by His Spirit to the sufferers for whose restoration I long with an entensity I can feel in no other subject.

CHAPTER I.

MY EARLY LIFE.

I was born October 23, 1835, in Cambridge-port, a suburb of the city of Boston, of Protestant parents who had emigrated shortly before from the North of Ireland. My mother I shall always remember as a plain, old-fashioned Methodist. She brought her religion with her from the county Fermanagh, the cradle of Irish Methodism, and she died in possession of the hope it imparts. My father, in his earlier years, was warm-hearted and mirthful. He was quick to catch and expose the ludicrous side of any subject, and was noted for having more than an ordinary share of that power of quick, pungent repartee so characteristic of his countrymen. Had his mind been thoroughly cultured, I believe he would have been noted for brilliant parts. But, in him, the religious element ran low, and, alas, all through life, he showed much weakness in the presence of the cursed strong drink; a fact that elicited many a sigh from my mother's heart, and gave serious trouble to the family. It was spasmodic, however, and did not hinder him from raising a large family in comparative comfort. I allude to this matter because I have reason to believe that if I fell heir to some of my father's better qualities, I also inherited *the whole* of his besetting weakness.

My parents, while I was yet a child, moved from Boston to the County of Huron, Upper Canada, where they had a number of relatives. In a few years they again removed: this time to Nashville, Tenn. Here life began to dawn upon me, and with the happy abandon of youth I enjoyed to the full the bright, sunny hours. Being somewhat of a favorite with my father he determined that I should be a scholar, and, being sent to a private school, my poor curly head was crammed with a mighty mass of knowledge—useful and ornamental; largely the latter. At the age of twelve I think it would be hard to find a boy who carried a larger bundle of books to school every morning, or who brought away at last less definite understanding of many of the subjects studied. However, I survived it, and contrived during the more thoughtful study of after years to disentangle in my mind the results of a hot-house system of education.

I need not take up space here in recounting what I saw of slavery in its palmy days, but I may say that even that far back my boyish eyes could plainly perceive that hatred of the North which culminated in the Great Rebellion. While we lived in Nashville several important public events transpired: After a severe contest James K. Polk was elected President, the foundation of the Court House was laid on Capitol Hill, and the first ground was broken in the construction of the present Nashville and Chattanooga Ry., all occuring about the year 1844, and considered great matters in that day.

That railways were much wanted, may be inferred from the fact that when we were forced to leave Tennessee for Canada in 1844 for the sake of father's health, it was necessary to travel from Cincinnati to Toledo by canal-boat, nearly a week being consumed on the journey.

CHAPTER II.

EARLY LIFE ON THE FARM.

As hinted at the close of the preceding chapter, our family turned its steps northward, in the early summer of 1844 in search of health for my father. Having engaged in various pursuits, he now determined to become a farmer; the first step being to purchase a section of land in Goderich township, County Huron, Upper Canada, about eight miles from Goderich, the County-town.

Our "farm" consisted of five acres of cleared land; all the rest being dense hard-wood forest. Although my father worked hard he never became very expert either as a woodsman or a farmer, and nearly all the "clearing" fell to the lot of my two elder brothers and myself. Most of it fell to my share, as the brothers mentioned soon left to work at the printing business which they had partially learned at Nashville. I was always willing to work, and taking kindly to the axe soon became expert in that branch of labor. Our life was, necessarily, somewhat rough, but what we lacked in refinement was more than made up in hearty good will. Our fare was not very luxurious, and it was sometimes a little scant; but the fresh air, with hard work and exuberant spirits enabled us to bring to the food prepared by the loving hands of one now a saint in Heaven a keenness of appetite which is the best of sauces. Taken altogether, those early pioneer times were amongst the most pleasant any of us have ever spent since.

There was a sociability; a free intercourse between neighbors in those early days which has disappeared long since. From far and near it was the custom to gather the people together to erect houses and barns, and "log," etc., the fun of the thing being in almost as much request as the work done. These gatherings generally brought the stout lads and buxom lasses into a dance the night following; and bad whisky was always supplied in abundance. At one of these mischievous affairs I first learned to drink to excess, although I did nothing like regular drinking for years afterwards.

But I soon discovered that farming was not to be my work for life. Being deprived of many of the privileges enjoyed by the young men of our day in the way of self-culture, I read the few books we had in our library until I could find little or nothing in them that I had not learned " by heart," and then begged the reading of any stray volume I could hear of any neighbor having. I certainly scraped together a wonderfully quaint sort of literary knowledge; but, as I look back at it there can be no doubt that the very paucity of books from which I thought I suffered was, in some respects, a great benefit.

And then in the warm Sunday mornings in early summer as I rambled in the grand old maple woods, saw the oriole threading the green foliage with gold, inhaled the sweet, subtle scent of the wild violet, and felt my ardent young soul entering into harmony with Nature, I discovered that there was an ideal life to be enjoyed in the

yond my present contracted sphere, and
break away I might be able to exchange
for—unknown bliss. I wanted to be
 to make the acquaintance, through their
who had accomplished much in the world.
the day might come when I could do
e world of letters myself.

n my only living parent, was nothing loth
 aspirations, and it needed but little
t his consent to leave the old farm in
and fortune. It caused me a severe pang
e was creeping on him, but we both
l be for the best.

CHAPTER III.

A PRINTER'S APPRENTICE.

Well do I remember the morning that I started out with my old father's benediction resting on me for the town of Goderich, eight miles distant, where my brother George and a partner had a printing-office in which I was to learn the trade. How fresh my spirits were! How elastic my step! What an ambition stirred within me to show what a farmer's boy could do, when I had acquired all the knowledge I intended to obtain.

I took very naturally to the printer's trade. There was a literary atmosphere about the office that delighted me, and then, for the first time, I could enter upon a more systematic course of self-culture than ever before. There was a little library in town, and after I had read through it, I began to purchase books for myself. The hours which are spent by most of the apprentices of the present day in worse than idleness were by me applied to hard study, and all my pocket-money nearly, went for books.

As an educational privilege I enjoyed at this time the excellent training for a young man of taking part in a debating club, most of the members of which were more advanced in scholarship than myself. I have to smile, sometimes, when I remember the perfect confidence with which the young man tackled any and every subject that came up for discussion.

At this time, and for years afterwards I was a total abstainer from all stimulants. Ah me! those early days had many bright spots in them. Student though I was. I soon learned to love Nature passionately, and my own heart seemed to beat responsive to her changeful moods. Often in the calm, beautiful mornings—and where are they more lovely—I have waded the river, and climbing up the opposite hill through a thicket of shrubbery laden with scented dew, stood at last on the bare summit, in presence of a scene calculated to enrapture any ardent young soul. Westward was the broad lake Huron, a watery mirror as far as the eye could reach—streaked with immense belts of green and blue and grey and only rippled with the long line of sparkles in the wake of a flying wild-duck ; away up east and southeast stretched the beautiful Maitland between banks lovely as were ever sung by poet, and as I gazed, trying to take in the beautiful picture, behold ! Aurora, goddess of the morning, attended by her bright train, ushered in the new-born day, as the first rays of the rising sun shed a sudden glory over the scene.

Those were pleasant days, taken altogether ; and if they were spent without any very definite purpose, I can, looking back at them, see nothing calculated to create feelings of remorse. There was certainly nothing boisterously wicked in my life as an apprentice.

CHAPTER IV.

CONVERSION AND MARRIAGE.

All through my young life were convictions of the necessity of a change of heart, at times quite pungent. I knew quite well that I was a sinner, and yet I put off the period of becoming reconciled with God through the merits of Christ's atonement until my twentieth year. The night the resolve was made is vividly impressed on my memory. It was at a protracted meeting which was held in the old frame Wesleyan Methodist Church on North street.* As I entered, Rev. Geo. Cochrane, now Missionary to Japan, was preaching, and ere I took my seat a thrill shot through me—a feeling of indescribable awe. God was there, and I felt at once that I must give my heart to him. Going to the altar with the seekers, I earnestly sought the pardon of my sins. The blackness of despair seemed to settle down upon me, and for three days and nights I lived in an agony of prayer. But, at last, in my own little bed-room, while reading a few well-directed words by a writer who knew exactly what to say to one in my condition, the light dawned suddenly upon my mind, and almost ere I was aware of it I

---

*The Wesleyan Methodist Church of Canada is meant. It was similar to the British Wesleyan body, and quite distinct from what is known as the Wesleyan Methodist Connection of the United States.

was a believer in Christ as my personal Saviour. Blessed hour! I never, from that time to this, doubted for a moment that I was converted then and there.

Being naturally of a warm, impulsive nature, I was full of zeal in the cause of the Master, for whose glory I determined to devote my life.

A young men's prayer-meeting was established in connection with the church, and we had glorious times. Several who are now standing steadfast as Christians date their spiritual birth from this period.

Through the exercise of whatever talents I was possessed of I was soon advanced to the position of class-leader, and afterwards to that of local preacher and trustee. For a number of years I filled these trusts with all the ability and energy I possessed. They were truly happy times, and as I look back upon them it is like gazing at a patch of brilliant sunshine through a murky, tangled, shadowy belt of forest.

Let the reader remember this brief statement of the religious joys that blessed my young manhood while perusing the dark record that follows.

About a year after my conversion, and when I was 21 years of age I married one who was then and is now a sincere Christian woman. We loved each other, and although our start in life was humble, we felt confident that strong hands and willing hearts would, with the blessing of God. enable us to establish a thoroughly Christian household, and secure a reasonable share of the world's prosperity. We anticipated nothing but a continuance of the happy contentedness that animated our hearts.

And we *would* have prospered had it not been for the one Accursed Thing that came to blight our young hopes and sweep away everything that was dear to us with remorseless cruelty. Alas! alas! how many thousands of bright homes have been destroyed by the same monster of iniquity. Many who read these lines will, may be, shed a tear as they look back in their own lives to just such an experience as ours has been. May all such come out of their awful trouble as we have done!

CHAPTER V.

MY FIRST WRONG STEP.

After I had been working for a number of years in my brother's office, it changed hands, and the old editor—Thomas McQueen, a great genius in his way—came back to it. One day he sent in a book notice of the Manual of Phonography, recommending young printers to learn the art. I determined at once to acquire what promised to be such a great help to me, and by constant study and practice became a somewhat efficient shorthand reporter.

Mr. McQueen took a liking to the printer boy, and fanned the flame of ambition in my breast to become a self-made journalist. How much, sometimes, a single word can do towards making or marring our fortunes.

One evening Mr. McQ. asked me into his "sanctum" and told me that as he believed the County seat question had been settled in our sister County of Bruce, I ought to go at once and start a paper in the new County-town. I had submitted several papers for his criticism, besides publishing several articles in the *Signal*, and he knew just what I could do. His decision that I was well able to write my own editorial articles, pleased me not a little.

I demurred, on account of youth and inexperience;

but he would take no denial—not only urging me to embark in the enterprise, but furnishing the necessary means until I could repay it, without interest.

Accordingly, all arrangements being made, my wife and I, in the winter of 1860-61 moved to Walkerton, the newly-fledged County-town. The "Town" consisted of about fifty houses built in a narrow valley between two high hills, a river-course having decided such a narrow position for the future metropolis. It was, as I gazed down on it in disgust from one of the hills, just about as unlikely a place to acquire literary eminence in as one could well imagine—the only redeeming feature being a fine agricultural country around the village.

However, undaunted, I went to work and soon had the unbounded satisfaction of seeing my first editorial in my own paper; and I had a pretty good opinion of it too, but after reading it several times I noticed that it did not by any means appear so bright and sparkling.

I can never forget that village. It had its various cliques, and society-grades, and "sets" all as clearly-defined as in any city. In winter there was some show of business, but in the long summer months the "town" went into a sort of drowsy sleep. Lack of business permitted the shopkeepers and their assistants to sit on goods boxes on the sidewalk and talk politics with the citizens, or to drink liquor. The liquor traffic, I noticed, flourished at all times.

I soon became disgusted with a place where there were, during certain seasons, seven Sundays a week; with the state of Society, and with my surroundings generally; and very soon felt that it was going to be a hard task to wait for the prosperity which was so far away.

And then I made my first great mistake in life: Our Methodist preacher, Rev. J. Hutchinson, came to me shortly after we had settled and asked me to fill a country Sabbath appointment for him. I promised him I would try. But, when the great cross came I failed. My supporters were nearly all rigid Presbyterians. How dare I acknowledge before them that I was a Methodist local-preacher by discharging this duty? And then too, I argued, why should I preach? If it had been my calling, would not the Canadian Conference have accepted me when I offered myself, instead of rejecting me on the plea that I was a married man? How easily we can justify ourselves in wrongdoing. I made it clear to my own mind that the duty laid upon me was too severe, and so I refused to fill the little appointment.

Ah me! that was an evil decision. God wanted me to stand up amongst so much of wickedness and vice as there was in that place, and be a true witness for Jesus, and I defiantly refused. Then the Lord withdrew his Spirit, and how I have suffered in consequence of that one rebellious act only God and my own soul can know. The act would appear to be a trivial one, almost, and yet it involved for me a principle of vital importance. It was a point where two roads diverged. I took the wrong road.

Had I stood up nobly for Christ, then, as I ought to have done—as the Spirit of God urged me—all would have been well, and instead of suffering the untold agony of after years, no doubt my life would have been devoted to the cause of God and humanity.

How many wrecked human lives can be plainly traced back to a similar starting point. I have no doubt these lines will be read by hundreds who will pause a moment to declare, if only to their own hearts: "Yes! if I had not failed when that clearly-defined duty came up—or, if I had not made that *one* false step, how different it would all have been." Oh! the Might Have Been; how it comes sighing in minor cadences through the memory of those who have sinned and suffered, and who have, by that very suffering, acquired the awful power of extracting the unutterable melancholy there is in Nature, however great the degree of happiness that may be ultimately restored to them!

Those who understand these matters, will not be surprised in the least when I inform them that soon after this event I felt that something had gone out of my life. There was an abiding sense of incompleteness; of loss. And well there might be, for a sweet link had disappeared from the chain of existence; not to be found and fully restored for sixteen long years freighted with sorrow and sin.

I tried to fill up the void with literature, but philosophy failed to feed the hungry soul. Lighter literature seemed but a bitter mockery; the veriest dust and ashes in the mouth. Then, in order to assist in whiling away the weary hours of inactivity, *I learned to use Tobacco.* I took to the pipe easily, and soon came to love it very dearly.

This was my first step downward, after passing the

turning-point. It is but one step from tobacco to liquor. Smoking and drinking are inseparable companions, the world over. I venture to assert boldly that nothing can so naturally quench the thirst caused by smoking as beer. When a young man learns to smoke, look out for the saloon : it is not very far distant. I must have commenced using tobacco in a fit of desperation. for I disliked the habit: and I may say that for over fifteen years I was disgusted with myself for having acquired it. I never could read a passage in the Bible with tobacco in my mouth. and, especially of late years, I felt the use of the poisonous weed to be a standing personal defilement. How I got finally rid of it will be related farther on.

Tobacco using, we are told. benumbs the moral sense. I know it did in my case. Up to this time I had been strictly teetotal on the temperance question : but I soon began to think it was useless to be so strict. Other professed Christians could use liquor moderately, why could not I? The Siren came and placed the wine cup in my hand, and I drank, not deeply at first, but enough to start me adrift in the direction of a drunkard's awful hell. If I could persuade myself that no harm would come of it; my wife, with Love's swift instinct, felt already the coming of the awful cloud that was to overshadow our young lives. If I apprehended any danger myse'f, I succeeded in laughing away my heart-felt convictions.

CHAPTER VI.

MY EDITORIAL CAREER.

Our stay in Walkerton only lasted about two years. My friend McQueen, dying, left the *Signal* without an editor, and I was induced to purchase it and assume the position I so much desired as its conductor. As all our old friends lived in and near Goderich, we were most comfortably situated, in regard to our social relations. In other respects, too, we prospered for a time. Business went well, the public smiled upon my literary efforts, and we looked forward to a happy and useful life. Popular applause is a sweet thing to an ardent, aspiring young man; but it is exceedingly dangerous. To be told that there is hardly any position that he may not attain to, may have some foundation in truth; and yet, if it does nothing worse, it creates an undue excitement of faculties of the mind which require no stimulus.

I was ambitious to secure a front place, if possible, in the race for fame. Even that, it seems to me was quite laudable, had I walked in the way my God desired I should; but I had made the first misstep and there was less difficulty about taking the second.

Being naturally light-hearted and generous, I soon formed intimate friendships with the witty and loose-living "men about town," who were always ready to laugh at my humorous sallies, and to drink at my expense. I am sorry to say that in the course of a few years I had learned to love the society to be found in the billiard-hall and the tavern, better than that of my old church friends, and by degrees, although keeping up a formal connection with the Church, I became thoroughly alienated in heart.

My connection with Canadian politics did not mend matters much. Somehow, from the first, there seemed to be one election after another in rapid succession, each, apparently, more exciting than the last ; and at the bottom of the turmoil, and ribaldry, and corruption, was always sure to be found an unlimited supply of strong drink. I saw many of the noblest young men of the country sink through this cause, and I never can think of this portion of my experience without a shudder. That I should escape the foul contagion, situated as I was would have been impossible. Link after link The Devil's Chain was forged and wound round me, dragging me down to the infamy of the drunkard's career.

A country editor who is at all popular, and who likes liquor-drinking and its associations, is in a very dangerous place. He is, it may be, generously disposed, and as he is continually conferring little favors to individuals through his paper for which no money equivalent is offered or expected, there is, every day of his life almost, a number of invitations to imbibe with those thus benefited, and if the temptation is given way to the tendency is to demoralization ; it is safe to say that the cause of such a man is downward. This has undoubtedly been the bane of many of the most talented young men of the country. Another thing that enters largely into the life of the editor of a country paper grows out of the fact that, during a considerable portion of the year, all the mental excitement he has is when his sheet is being prepared for the press. As soon as his week's work is accomplished, he is apt to suffer a period of depression which nothing in his surroundings is calculated to dispel —except the ever-ready whiskey or brandy bottle. That is the rock upon which many a fair young life has been wrecked. It would seem that such a simple course could hardly produce such awful effects, and yet I have no doubt numbers who read this will be able to attribute their downfall to just such an influence. Ah, me! I learned the fatal secret that there is a power in strong drink, at first, to drive off "dull care," to unloose the fancy to stimulate every flagging power of the being. Why suffer from depression of spirits when immunity could be purchased so cheaply? Why write with fingers of lead, when I could easily secure the means of sending the warm blood bounding with a quickened pulsation through every vein—opening up to the enraptured vision all that heated imagination could paint or heart desire.

I enjoyed the dreamy elysium of such a life in the society of those who were of my own way of thinking for several years. Poor fellows! some of them lie in the Goderich Cemetery, murdered by the accursed Destroyer while yet in the hey-day of their early manhood, while others are wanderers far from the scenes of our wicked revelry. I look back upon this period of my life with peculiar horror. I was deliberately poisoning my whole being—body and soul—with alcohol.

During particularly dull days and evenings it was the practice of our party to meet in some saloon or grocery and there while away the hours in playing various games for beer, and engaging in such conversation as we considered witty and amusing. Saturday evening was a favorite time for such gatherings, as the bars being virtually closed on Saturday evening, and the Sabbath rendered it not quite so easy to procure stimulant; hence it was deemed advisable to drink as much as possible the evening before. Thus the eve of the holy Sabbath was profaned by orgies which disinclined any who indulged in them from worship next day.

All this sort of life kept up a constant drain upon my purse, and gradually, but very surely, the means which should have been held for business or gone for home comforts and necessaries, were expended to prove to a number of misguided associates that I was a man of noble feelings and generous instincts. It is true I often suffered a pang when I saw my family becoming pinched for necessary articles, while the liquor-dealer could have the very best of all there was to be had; but such is the terrible glamor of intemperance, that the outraged and enfeebled moral sense becomes, at last, unable to see the full enormity of the crime committed. I know that was the case with myself, and furthermore, I soon came to lose all power to resist the tide that was bearing me so surely to destruction.

All this time I was sinning and repenting; but gradually losing my grasp on every religious or moral aid to a better life. My friends saw with horror the awful fate that seemed to lie before me, and, as far as they dared interfere, endeavored to save me. I fairly loathed myself, and yet, somehow, it seemed impossible to stop.

And those, too, who had been my loving companions in the Church; how their hearts yearned over the poor sinful wanderer! How earnestly they prayed that the Lord would bring me back to Christ! I could not realize *then* what they suffered on my account, but I can *now*, thank God.

CHAPTER VII.

MY DOWNFALL.

There came a time at last when prudence, and decency, and Christian propriety were all thrust rudely aside and I appeared upon the street in broad day light in a state of intoxication; not once or twice, merely, but several times. Even then, the devil persuaded me, that it was merely an outbreak of the eccentricity which sometimes accompanies true talent. But one evening, when my eldest daughter, a sweet little girl, came home bathed in tears and declared amidst heart-breaking sobs that she could go no more to school, because the girls pointed at her, and refused to associate with her because she was *a drunkard's child*, I suddenly awoke to a full sense of the fact that I was a DRUNKARD! O! merciful God! what a horror there was in the very name! And to feel in my soul that I deserved it—that if I was to be cast out of the pale of respectable society it was but right. In the whole course of my life I do not think I have suffered such agony as was condensed into that hour.

I felt then that I had parted with the last semblance of true Christianity, and that it was my imperative duty to withdraw from the Church, rather than to wait to be turned out by legal action. Next morning, therefore, I wrote out a request that my name should be stricken from the records of the Church of my mother. I remember the scene well: the appearance of the paper, the pen, the surroundings of the little editorial room where I had formerly spent so many happy hours; and as I signed my name to the paper, after assigning the true reason for taking such a step, I felt that I had subscribed my own death-warrant—of both body and soul. I sent the note to our pastor, Rev. W. H. Poole, and the next Sabbath being the occasion of a quarterly meeting, it was read before the whole membership. Although not present, I felt the degradation bitterly—all the more because I knew that it was well deserved. I afterwards learned that there was not a dry eye in the church when the letter was read; but that fact had no power to move me out of the course I intended to pursue.

Now I was free from all restraint, and could do just as I pleased. I could get drunk every day if I chose. It was the grim freedom that comes from desperation; yet, such as it was I enjoyed it to the uttermost. Recklessness and Ruin are twins. I very soon discovered that fact, for my descent from this point was one of fearful rapidity. I need not enter into details, beyond stating that for months, excepting an occasional spasm of repentance, I never drew a really sober breath. Inebriety became, with me, a disease.

Intemperance and poverty go hand in hand. Few young men had better opportunities for building up a fortune than I, and yet there I was so fully under the control of appetite that I saw my business slipping away from me without being able, through moral and physical weakness to avert the impending destruction.

I tried to recover myself. Yes, I endeavored by ever-weakening spasms of effort to recover a hold of my business. And oh! how hard I tried to escape from the bondage of drink. I went to the doctor and the clergyman; but they both failed me, for neither of them knew just how I could be saved. I wearied out the patience of my friends with promises which were broken almost as soon as made. I have wept like a child in my utter helplessness, and then determined that I would reform. A week or two of sobriety, and then a little leak of cider, ginger-wine, etc., would bring back the full tide of drunkenness. On one occasion I went so far in my agony as to write a pledge on the fly-leaf of our family-Bible, and sign it, with the avowed determination of never touching liquor while it remained there. Did I keep to my resolution? Alas, before one week had passed, I knew I should have to recommence my old career, and in order to satisfy my poor abused, dying conscience, in some degree, *I tore the leaf out of the book!* My dear reader, when you hear the assertion that there is nothing in this world that can make a man do such mean things as alcohol urges him to do, believe it—for it is true!

Alcohol acts upon its victims in various ways. Some are rendered savage by it; some foolish, simply; others stupid. With me there was at first an intense degree of mental excitement, followed, at a later stage—especially if I went from a heated room to the open air—by an irresistible tendency to sleep; no matter where I might be at the time. When it is remembered that I became intoxicated at every favorable opportunity, it will not be wondered at that I had some very narrow escapes from instant death. Several times, late on stormy winter nights, I should have died, undoubtedly, in the snow where I had fallen, had it not been for the frantic efforts of my faithful Newfoundland dog, who, by some means, contrived to rouse me to action ere the last deep sleep had overtaken me. Poor Victor, you were better to me than many of my old comrades! On another occasion I drove a horse and buggy—or, rather, the horse picked his own way—for some ten or twelve miles on a dark night, down a steep hill, across a river-bridge, up another hill and several miles beyond. When my senses came back in a dazed sort of way, I had great difficulty in finding out where I was, or the direction home. It was of the great mercy of God that, in some way, I was not cut down in the midst of my wickedness. I sometimes think God hates, if possible, to allow a drunkard to die in his sins, above all other men, without giving them repeated opportunities for repentance, knowing that it drags after it such a hideous trail of sin and misery and crime.

One after another I tried the various temperance organizations, only to find that each proved a failure. What was there in a mere pledge that could meet an appetite for stimulants such as mine? I broke through pledges as though they had been but spiders' webs; and my little stock of resistance became less and less with each failure. I know a sense of honor should have carried me through; but a drunkard has no honor, and hence, is beyond the reach of ordinary influences.

While money lasted, I had quite a number of friends;

for, desiring to be accounted a real good-fellow, I was always liberal in treating my companions. But when, through my business dropping off, money was not by any means so plentiful, I realized at once a great change in my quondam friends. They at once put on an air of superior virtue, and with a "Poor Cox, how I pity him!" they gave me the cold shoulder. And many of my dear friends, the hotel and saloon keepers did not seem to relish my frequent visits. Although I had invested with them my glorious young ambition, my means—my very soul's salvation—they could coldly hint that "it would be better for me to be doing something for my suffering family." Thank God, I do not need now to grind my teeth in helpless agony as I think of the indignities then heaped upon me. But when I think that so many of my dear brethren in suffering are sitting in just such a wretched state, I can hardly wait till I make an effort to rescue them from a bondage cruel to endure, and yet so easy to escape from when the way is made plain.

I have hinted that my business began to go down. Of course, where both the ability and the inclination to attend to such matters was absent, want of confidence on the part of my creditors soon brought about the inevitable collapse. One day I went home and found the gaunt wolf of Famine staring in at the door. There was nothing for my wife and children to eat. O! how sincerely I ask our heavenly Father to bless the friend who, while others were false, and cruel, stepped between my family and absolute starvation.

CHAPTER VIII.

LIFE IN CHICAGO.

That my career in Goderich had terminated was but too evident. No matter how brilliant my opportunities were, or how dear the old place and its sweet associations was to my heart, the time had come when I must bid it adieu, and go—I hardly cared where. I believe in my soul there is a special Providence, which, if we follow its leading, directs our steps in the *only* safe direction. I am sure it was so in my case. It would seem that, of all places in the wide world in which to seek for reformation from the habit of intemperance, a great city would be the very worst; and yet, if the reader will carefully peruse what follows, the wonder-working power of God will, I trust, be made manifest.

I hardly know how it got into my beclouded brain that I should go to Chicago, but, somehow, the impression was there as clearly as was the idea that I must leave my old home. In the hope that any change might be for the better, I made what preparations I could, borrowed a few dollars to pay my passage by water, and bidding adieu to my stricken household, I started out to seek my fortune in the West. My wife had a faint hope that I might reform, and my dear pastor of better times, Rev. W. H. Poole, declared that too many earnest prayers had been offered to God on my behalf to permit of my being lost. It was, under the circumstances, a wonderful degree of faith. Beyond these two I do not believe another soul expected to see me alive again.

I went away with a hard, crushing bitterness at my heart. As the shores of home receded from view, and the truth flashed upon me with awful force that henceforth I should be a wanderer and an alien, I cursed those who had hastened to take advantage of my weakness with the terrible maledictions which spring so easily to the lips of a man in my deplorable condition.

I landed in the city of Chicago on the 26th day of July, 1871, with the sum of $4.60 in my pocket. Fresh from a quiet country town, where the current of ordinary life flows along so sluggishly, no wonder I was somewhat stunned by the rush and bustle and confusion of the great metropolis of the West. Sick in body; broken in spirit; low in purse; alone in a crowd. Put all these things together, and you have an aggregate of wretchedness such as I experienced in Chicago. What was I to do? I was too long out of practice to do much at the mechanical part of my business, while my habits rendered anything better out of the question. I very soon found that I could do no better than drift along in a nomadic sort of way, earning what little I could, and learning from others as miserable as myself those poor makeshifts that enter so largely into that kind of life.

In one way or another I dragged through the summer, drinking incessantly and never having any sum worth sending home. Bad as I was, I suffered extremely when thoughts of wife and children arose in my mind. When the news came to me that another son had been born into our family, I felt very unequal to any further responsibility, judging from the past. It seemed to widen the breach between me and all hope of ever regaining a position where I could do anything for those whom I was called upon by every tie to cherish and protect.

Then came the great Chicago fire, in October, 1871. That great calamity has been described so often and so well, that I need not stop here to enter into particulars concerning it. One thing is certain: it was the sublimest sight a human being can ever witness. I carried my trunk through the greater portion of the burning "North Side," but had to abandon it at last—glad to escape with life.

Still clinging to the city after the fire I settled down a little better to work for a while, but I found that I was deficient in endurance on account of the strain that had been put upon my vital powers, and to heighten my wretchedness, during the fall and early winter my limbs became so swollen as to render me almost helpless. When I saw at last that I could not work steadily I felt like giving up in despair. Knowing where temporary relief could be had, I flew to the bottle, and there found relief from my misery by drowning it in copious draughts of villainous whisky.

Such a life could have but one ending. Canadian whisky was destructive; but how much more so the vile stuff sold in low-grade Chicago saloons! No living man could stand it. I kept on at it, however, until the morning of January 22, 1872, when my employer very properly discharged me on account of inattention to business through drink.

I wended my way to a saloon on West Madison street, and contrived to spend or lose every cent I had about me, before nine o'clock in the evening.

CHAPTER IX.

"OUT OF THE DEPTHS."

About 11 o'clock of that night of January 22, 1872, it would be difficult to find in all the cold, cruel city of Chicago a more pitiful object than I was. The night was a bitterly cold one, and as the wind struck me it seemed to pierce to the very marrow. I had on no underclothing. My covering consisted of an old summer suit utterly unfit for such a season, and my feet were barely covered by a pair of worn old shoes.

But worse still my heart was cold. Last of all Hope had fled, and there I was, in the heart of a great city alone, moneyless, homeless, friendless. Giant Despair seized me and I seemed almost ready to give up the unequal strife. I asked the pale, cold marble churches if no man cared for my soul; I looked up at the grand business palaces and wondered that I could not have enough to procure food and warmth. And then as I walked the deserted streets at midnight there went up from the heart of the poor wanderer "OUT OF THE DEPTHS" a cry for help that God must have heard. Not knowing anything better to do, I explained my circumstances to a policeman, and asked him if there was any place in the city where men so situated could get a night's lodging. He gave me a ticket for admittance during the remainder of that night at a so-called "Police Lodging-house," on Union street. Presenting my ticket I was admitted to a Chamber of Horrors, such as I had never before heard or read of. Had it not been a matter of life or death with me, I should certainly have turned back into the darkness and cold, but I thought I could stand it until morning and so determined to make the attempt. The room was the full length of the building, there was no stove in it, and the miserable ones who tarried there for the night were expected to sleep on a bare shelf-like platform without a particle of covering, beyond their ragged clothing. There they lay, thick as herrings in a row, rendering the air poisonous with their foul breath, and vocal with blasphemy. It seemed to me as though Nemesis had, with a giant hand, raked every alley and slum of the city and thrown the contents here.

What an awful night it was! I shall never lose a single detail of its unutterable horror while memory holds true to its office. As I lay there shivering I thought: And has it come to this at last. Has the man who was to have done something in the world descended so low that he must herd with the vilest off-scourings of the earth? How soon can one die if this must be the mode of living?

At last the 23d of January dawned—a day to be held in remembrance while life lasts, on account of the infinite mercy of God. At the first appearance of daylight we were driven forth by the brutal keeper of the shameful den, and I was glad to breathe once more the pure air, if it was cold.

That was a bitter, freezing morning. Tired, sick, wretched, I stepped out beneath the paling stars. The greatest want I experienced—more than food, or warmth, or rest, much as I needed these—was *drink* ; something to satisfy the craving for stimulants. Wandering down to Canal street, near Madison, to my great joy I found that a saloon kept by a friend of mine was open ; and he had his place well warmed up. What a heaven it seemed ! I thought I could never absorb enough of the life-giving heat. How is it that in the great emergencies of our lives, the mind has such a trick of taking note of the minutest details of our surroundings ? I can recall the whole scene as vividly as though nothing else had ever been imprinted on my memory : The hot stove, the people in the room, the cheap pictures on the wall, the various little objects to be met in such places—all passes in review. I took an old letter or two out of my pocket and tried to read them in an off-hand way, so that the man might not take me for a loafer altogether.

I sat there for about an hour: and in that hour I did all the serious thinking my poor racked brain was capable of. I knew right well that it had at last come to be a matter of life or death with me. If I continued in my drinking course, there was nothing for me, in less than a month, but the city hospital and the pauper's grave. If I stopped short—well, I might at least die sober. It was useless for me to seek work, for I was too feeble to do anything in the shape of labor, and there seemed only one chance for me.

At last, with my mind fully made up, I stepped up to the counter and telling the proprietor of the saloon I had no money, asked him if he would give me a drink of liquor to quench my raging thirst. He handed me the whisky-bottle and I poured out at least three-fouths of a glassful of the fiery liquid and drank it down. And then, as I returned the empty glass to the counter, I said, *By the help of Almighty God, that is the last drop of liquor of any kind that will ever pass my lips!* That was four-and-a-half years ago. Oh! how sincerely I praise the name of Him who has enabled me to keep that vow intact to the present time. I shall not attempt to analyze the process by which I made up my mind to reform. It seems to miraculous that a man who had fallen so low could be induced to make the attempt. It was a direct miracle of divine grace rescuing fallen humanity. When I cried to the Lord out of the depths He delivered me. It is because of my faith that there is a like deliverance for every sufferer who will seek it in the same way that I urge upon ienbriates everywhere the *hopefulness* of their boldly taking the same step.

Although I had done what I could, thus far, I was satisfied that I required speedy succor if I was to be saved; but where it would come from was the problem. Dear reader, do you believe in an overruling Providence? I do. As I stood there, not knowing where to turn my anxious steps, God threw out to me a little Providential thread, by following which I was led into a place of safety. I remembered having some conversation a few days before with regard to the Washingtonian Home. I determined to seek admittance to that institution, and accordingly set out in search of it. I found that it was situated on Madison street, opposite Union Park, about one and a half miles distant. Although I started at once, I was so enfeebled that it took me until nearly noon to get to the neighborhood of the Home. I did not go in directly—my heart failing me when I got in sight of it. Entering a saloon a short distance down on the opposite side of the street, I sat down for a last think.

I was in a poor condition for lucid thought; but the more I dwelt upon the matter, the more thoroughly I was convinced that the step suggested to me was the right one. When a man finds himself in such a desperate strait, the sooner he gets rid of pride and conventional prejudices the better.

At length I entered the Home, and found myself in the presence of the Superintendent, J. M. Van Court. He spoke kindly, but stated that it was necessary that my friends should secure payment of my board, or that some arrangement to that end should be made. Not knowing exactly who my friends were, or how I could muster enough strength to search for them, I told him I was helpless; but if he could save a fellow-man from destruction there was no time to lose. I do not know what predisposed Mr. Van Court in my favor; but he finally resolved to take me *on trial*, "For," said he, "with the dry New England twinkle in his eye, "I've "tried printers before, by the score, and not one of them "has succeeded in reforming."

Well, said I,—with a little spasm of doubt—I will be the one who will reform and stick to it. Heaven bless the man, who, behind the dry exterior of a New Englander, bears a heart as tender as any woman's! In admitting me to the Home contrary to the strict letter of the law he saved me from inevitable death.

CHAPTER X.

LIFE IN THE HOME.

The very fact that I sought the Washingtonian Home as a last asylum, in my extreme necessity, goes far towards indicating what kind of place it was. The building at that time was an old three-story frame—since replaced by a splendid edifice, I believe. It is governed by a board of directors and is always under the immediate charge of a superintendent and matron. It is, in fact, an inebriate asylum, and its inmates range from the unhappy victims of *delirum tremens,* placed there by their friends as a kind of forlorn hope, to men who deliberately present themselves for the purpose of making a desperate struggle to gain the victory over the fearful appetite for strong drink. In this class I have met men capable of filling any position demanding classical scholarship, thorough business training and general accomplishments of a high order. The wit, the poet, the ready writer, the orator, the child of genius; alas! alas! Only a percentage of these poor fellows, even at the last awful extremity, will consent to be saved. I witnessed some heart-rending scenes in the Home. Many, however, saved through this instrumentality, are to-day occupying places of honor and trust.

I entered the Home ill—so ill that the attendant physician pronounced me incurable, and urged my being sent to the city hospital. I hated to go there, and plead so strongly that it was not insisted upon. I had a feeling strong upon me that God did not want me to die yet, and the result proved I was right.

I sat in one spot most of the time for a week, simply because I was afraid to move about. Drinking men will know all about that feeling that makes one, when recovering from a debauch, afraid to approach a stairway for fear of falling, or dread to overstep the slightest obstruction, lest a tumble should follow. It is partial paralysis.

In a week or two my disease gave way before the medicines used, and I gradually gained strength. The warmth, the rest, the good, substantial food! How good they seemed after the whirl of inebriety!

At last sleep came to me; soft, sweet, refreshing: like that of an infant. Oh! the blessed boon of sleep undisturbed by the loathsome dreams of debauchery! The ability to sleep seemed to be better medicine for mind and body than anything else.

We had meetings in the chapel of the Home Wednesday and Sunday evenings. On these occasions I expressed my determination to make a thorough reformation of it, by God's help, and several times I was blamed by the other inmates for being too radical; but I believe I was right. Many of the poor fellows who refused to take strong ground are now hopeless wrecks. I was by no means a religious man at this time, but there was in connection with my experience a degree of tenderness of heart akin to religious emotion. Frequently during those days of crawling back to life I bowed in secret prayer, the burden of which was that I might be saved from intemperance. As the glamour of inebriety wore off I began to see the enormity of the sin of drunkenness. From that time forward I bore this sense of impurity in my heart, until I found relief through faith in the Sinner's Friend.

As I sat there thinking, thinking: of the past, the present, the future; there dawned upon me something at last that I can never write except in capital letters—a glorious HOPE! Hope, that embraced the welfare of my beloved ones, when I should be a reformed creature beyond peradventure—hope that I should sometime stand, head erect before my fellow-men, redeemed from the curse of drunkenness—a hope that somewhere in this glorious, golden West I should be able to make a home for the dear family I had so cruelly wronged.

I was six or seven weeks in the Home ere I wrote to my wife in Canada. Hitherto I had sent no relief to the family, and as I sobered the sense of shame at my heart made me fear to hear from them before I had forwarded some money in their dire necessity. My wife wrote to friends in Chicago who searched for me high and low; but not a trace of me could be found, and it was believed at last that I had sunk in the maelstrom of a great city's vice and misery. Hence, the joy with which the first letter home was hailed.

I became stronger each day, and began to long for some kind of steady employment. I determined to start right at the bottom of the ladder and work my way up. It was a good resolve, as I now look back at it. Let me urge it as strongly as possible upon all who are seeking reformation to go right to work at the first thing that presents itself, and stick to it. The temptation to return to drink is not half so strong when we are busy at work. I soon obtained a little employment at which I labored till June, 1872, when one day I met Charles Stevenson, a printer-friend, who invited me down to Aurora to work on Mr. Edward's great Directory of Chicago.

CHAPTER XI.

IN AURORA.

That same day I left for Aurora, Ill., expecting to be absent only about seven weeks. In a few days work commenced and went on rapidly till August, when the Chicago Directory was completed. In our office force of some forty hands most of the poor fellows drank up their wages as fast as they earned them, but I can truly say that I had not the slightest temptation to indulge. Indeed, the more I saw of liquor and its effects the more loathsome it became to me. I sent a little money home to my family each week, placing the balance of my wages in a savings bank, to meet the grand end I had in view. Having written previously for my family to come on, I went into Chicago on the 7th of August to meet them.

As the boat touched the dock and I leaped upon the deck, the reader may imagine the scene, as locked in each others' arms, the tears of gladness flowed from our eyes. The dead was alive—the old-time husband and father had come back again, and—*all was well.*

On clubbing together our little remaining funds, my wife and I found we would be very bare by the time we got to Aurora with our effects, and so I had to sell my much-loved library to a heartless shark of a second-hand dealer, for a mere tithe of what it had cost me. I felt this forced deprivation very much. To part with authors whom I had conversed with as to familiar friends in happier days, seemed to be the heaviest blow of the kind that had fallen upon me, and yet the pitiful sum it produced was necessary to help in our fresh start in life.

Gathering together what was left of our household effects, and with hearts determined not to be appalled at the difficulties lying before us, we traveled by rail to Aurora. Without any certainty of how work would be, I had determined to keep my flock from the vicious surroundings of a great city, in hopes that the way would brighten before us. I had rented a little house; but to place in it furniture and such utensils as were absolutely necessary to commence house-keeping in even the smallest way, was a problem very difficult to solve. Rather sad was that family " council of war," on ways and means, as my dear wife and I slowly paced up the shady side of the street on that hot August day. I thought at the time, and have often thought since, that the reformation of such a man as I was did not partake altogether of the romantic. In the temperance tale we are taught that the climax of interest is reached when the poor drunkard is fairly ushered into his new life. That may be true in a certain sense; but, as I look upon the matter, the greatest and noblest work has yet to be accomplished. You may conduct the man to the foot of the ladder and place his foot upon the bottom round, but how little of the work of reformation will be thus accomplished! Will the poor fellow climb through all the difficulties which beset him? Will he stand true as steel in the presence of fierce temptation?

It was a humble habitation into which I ushered my wife and little ones, and very humble were the surroundings, and yet this was "Home, sweet home." We were re-united, and I believe each member of the family was filled with an earnest desire and determination to spare no exertion to raise ourselves into a better position. With this courage in our hearts we could afford to laugh at the shaky condition of the furniture, and to pardon the many cracks in our stove when we tasted how good was the cooking it did. All this, no doubt, may seem very simple and foolish to those whose lives have always been happy and comfortable; but to those who are struggling to make a fresh start in life, it means a great deal.

For some weeks I had partial employment in the old office. Finally, however, work slackened and then gave out altogether, with the hope to cheer us that at some indefinite period it would be revived. What a weary time of waiting that was! Week after week passed away—six, seven, eight—and still nothing to do! That was my time of trial. There we were, in a land of plenty, to be sure; but strangers in a strange land, where cash in hand was the rule of trade, and our last dollar went long before relief came. I am satisfied that a hint of our condition to the good Christian people of Aurora would have brought immediate succor, and yet I have always been glad that hint was never uttered. As I sat there day after day, brooding over the awful condition into which I had brought my dear ones by my own folly, I was forced to endure a degree of remorse and shame and discouragement such as I had never felt before. I had made an honest effort at reformation, and, after all, we must go down under the pressure of grinding want. Where could I turn? What could I do? As I look back at that time, and the fierce struggle through which I passed, sitting helplessly idle when I longed for employment, I can see that it was the great Ordeal of my life. Many and many a time would I have sunk in despair had it not been for the presence of one who, standing faithfully by my side, pointed with steady faith to the better time that was surely coming. Oh! the holy confidence of the little half-sick pale-faced woman who proved so faithful and true in that dark hour! May God bless her.

Dear reader, since that time I have had much experience of drinking men, and one fact, above all others has affected my heart: When a man has gone down under the influence of strong drink; when all of former good has faded away; when cherished boon companions have turned their backs upon him, the last one to forsake the poor outcast is some mother, or daughter or wife. Nay, how seldom does the loving heart ever forsake the degraded one. Oh! save my husband! save my son! is the wail that has come up to me from many a bleeding heart.

At last the weary waiting came to an end. Work was resumed at the office, and the stream of life began to flow more cheerfully. That seemed to end the great struggle of our lives, for since that time work has been plentiful and the way clear at all times. Indeed, the indications of Providence became very clear. During the spring following, just as the last of our directory work was to close and the office be removed to Chicago, our foreman came in one evening and in a sneering way announced that Mr. Bailey, proprietor of the *Free Methodist*, then printed in Aurora, wanted a hand. Our office people generally hooted at the smallness of the job, but, thinking it might suit me, I quietly washed my hands and stepped over to see Mr. Bailey. In the conversation that followed I frankly told him what kind of man I had been and what I was trying to be. Something in the recital, I know not what, seemed to incline his heart towards me, and as we shook hands at parting I knew not only that I had obtained the situation, but secured a life-long friend.

That was a good step for me to take. In a few weeks Brother Bailey gave me the foremanship of the paper, and handed over the proof-reading and other office responsibilities which I have endeavored to meet in a spirit of faithfulness to the present day. The literary character of the paper just suited the bent of my mind, and as I had in the past studied up Methodistic theology pretty thoroughly, I felt very much at home. To Lewis Bailey and J. M. Y. Smith, both now gone to their reward, I owe a great deal—not for any *direct* good they did me so much as their quiet recognition that I was a member of the human family, and, as such, entitled to some regard in my sphere in life. If employer and employed always held towards each other such relations as did Brother Bailey and I, how much would the burden of business life be lightened! He said little or nothing to me on the subject of religion, which, perhaps, was the wisest course he could have taken. It was much better for me that my knowledge of the genius of Free Methodism should be gathered from the silent logic of Christian lives and the influence of what came under my observation in the columns of the paper. I can truly say that up to the period of his untimely death in December, 1873, Brother Bailey's intercourse with me was of the kind best calculated to heal the harsh wounds in my heart, and the months spent in the service of Sister Bailey, until the paper was transferred to its present proprietors were, I believe, fraught with mutual pleasure and profit.

On the 12th of August, 1874, *The Free Methodist* office became the property of its present proprietors, Messrs. Baker & Arnold, by purchase from Sister Bailey. It was decided by the new purchasers to remove the office from Aurora to Sycamore, Ill., which was done during August, 1874. I accompanied the office to Sycamore, in the capacity of foreman, and, taking a great liking to the little city on account of its beauty and thrift, I have tried to lay the foundation of a permanent home for my family. The Lord has, thus far, smiled upon our earnest efforts. With regard to the new proprietors and my relations to them, I am, of course, not free to say much; but it cannot be wrong to bear testimony to their universal kindness, and the constant pleasure I have experienced in their service. Indeed, our feelings towards each other have been those of brothers rather than the sort produced by mere dollar and cent arrangements.

CHAPTER XII.

MY SPIRITUAL RESTORATION.

From the fact that when I left off drink in Jan., 1872, to Aug., 1875, I made no special profession of Christianity, some have leaped to the conclusion that, after all, my reformation was nothing more than a most extraordinary exertion of human will. As the case will doubtless prove interesting to the Christian reader, it may be well to present somewhat fully the facts of my restoration to spiritual life.

Let the reader turn back to the description I have given of myself as I appeared on the morning of the 23d of January, 1872, and decide in his or her mind whether such a poor lost creature could possibly summon up *will power* enough to accomplish the enormous work of self-reformation. It is easy for people who are not under the slavery of appetite to declare that when the mind is fully made up and kept to the great point aimed at the blessed work is more than half accomplished. I have heard lecturers declare that it is the *first glass* that brings ruin back to soul and body under such circumstances; but what can these fine gentlemen and ladies know of the agony of the wretched man who is endeavoring to steel himself against taking that first glass when his whole being cries out for the accustomed stimulus with a degree of fierceness which will take no ordinary denial? What do they know of the power it takes to hold such an one to *any* lucid purpose? I had tried to reform many times before, under far more favorable circumstances, and yet each failure was worse than the last. On this occasion, however, sick, with fluttering heart and quivering nerves, and the whole weight of my degredation upon me, I was enabled to *stop, at once and forever!* I could no more have done that than I could have created a world.

No! no! the secret of the whole matter is here: There comes a time in the career of every drinking man when he is in a condition of awful *extremity*—when sunk in the depths, he sees vividly that it is a matter of life or death; that if he is not saved now he never will be. A God of infinite love and pity and tenderness beholds the wretched one in the horrible pit and miry clay. The poor drunkard cries to the only One able to save "out of the depths," and then He, who must hate of all things to see such a loathsome object die in his sin, hears that last despairing cry, and reaching away down, draws up the sinner and he is saved—God puts into him the ability to trample appetite under foot, and thus the way is open for his salvation. Nothing but the power of God can save a man in such a fearful extremity as I have described!

I felt this from the very dawn of final reformation, as it sprang up in my mind I recognized a spirit of tenderness such as I had not experienced for years. I felt certain that God pitied me, and that, I truly believe, was the dawning of my hope; for if he pitied me, he would surely help me out of the jaws of Hell.

From the first hour of my deliverance the Spirit of God was ever present, pleading with me to become a true Christian, and I can conscientiously say that there was an ever-growing purpose to listen to those sweet pleadings. I should have taken a stand at once as a Christian, and thus have given God glory for what had been done for me; but let the reader remember that, no matter what may have been the extent of former enjoyment, the mind of a man who sinks as low as I did becomes extremely dark, and less surprise will be experienced.

Right here I would like to allude to a matter of vital importance and one which should not, in my estimation, be left out of the discussion of temperance reformation: When a man with no special reference to Christianity, becomes reformed, and, purified from the last taint of alcohol, enters into the duties and responsibilities of a member of society once more, are not the restraints of honor, family pride, and a consciousness of integrity of purpose, perfect safeguards against his ever falling again? That is a question put by thousands who strongly desire to enjoy the full benefits of a life of temperance without having to bend the will—what there is of it—to the claims of Christianity. After having had much experience with such men, and having been able to watch their career, for a number of years, I have no hesitation in answering, No! Men sometimes start well. They cut of the indulgence of their appetite and declare that they are forever done with that which has blighted their lives. The principle that animates them is dogged determination allied with human pride. Now, to look at such persons, you would believe they were stable as the everlasting hills. It is not so, however; for, when the hour of great trial comes, the poor, frail human will gives way and down sinks the man who thought himself so strong. Let some great calamity arise—some downfall in business, the death of a very dear friend, or anything of the kind, and the result is almost inevitable. The poor fellow's props are all taken away, and he at once topples to his fall. No matter how long men may have stood the test—I have known them do so for years—if they persistently resist the claims of religion they will ultimately fall. I have seen some heart-breaking cases of this, some of which, with a few of an opposite character, will be related in another chapter.

Being well aware that the Christian was fully armed against any assault, and occupied a vantage ground that could never fail while a hold was retained of the Divine Arm, I made up my mind at last that I would seek the double-assurance promised in the Word of God.

From the nature of my calling it was my duty to read very carefully all the articles which passed through our paper, and as these mainly treated upon matters connected with vital religion, I was placed by the kind Providence that saved me thus far under the most favorable circumstances for discovering what my aching heart wanted to know. Often, as I have read an article embracing a deep experience of the things of God, which seemed to warm the soul into a blaze of spiritual life, I have laid the manuscript or proof down and asked myself the question, "Is that really so? if I were to comply with these conditions would I feel anything like that? What a blessed change it would be! Why, that was the kind of religion I longed for in the ardent days of my young manhood!"

As the months passed on I made up my mind at last that I would publicly embrace Christianity at the first favorable opportunity. I kept my own secret, however, not even letting my wife know the state of my feelings.

At this time we were attending a fashionable church, where the members who had the true ring of Christianity about them might be counted upon a very small scale, and where pride and formality held full sway over the great majority. Several times "revivals" were held in this church, but while I wished to possess a *respectable* kind of religion, I thought this was *too* respectable to satisfy the longings of my nature, and I could not, therefore, accept of it.

About the middle of August, 1875, the Free Methodist people erected in our town what they called a district tent, capable of accommodating two or three hundred people, for the purpose of holding religious meetings, several ministers from a distance being called upon to render assistance from time to time.

I listened to the preaching attentively. The doctrines explained were, as far as I could see, those of the Bible. The people were urged to come through a thorough conviction and repentance to the only Way of escape. It was held out that nothing short of a complete separation from the world and a complete, all-embracing consecration to the service of God could enable us to enter the Holy City at last. I believed every word of it! I had longed for such a religion in my early manhood. It was the religion of Wesley and his coadjutors. It fired the hearts of all moral reformers who had ever appeared upon the earth. It was the vital element of Christian holiness—the religion of the Bible.

And yet I had some serious objections. A people who held such close scriptural ideas with regard to dress, etc., must necessarily be unpopular and looked down upon by the masses of so-called respectable society, and this is far from being agreeable to the natural man. When one seriously begins to count the cost of living a life of self-denial and cross-bearing for Christ's sake, many things assume a new aspect.

But while I felt that I might be able to count all things but loss for the excellency of the knowledge of my blessed Saviour, there was one point upon which I foresaw great difficulty: If I joined these simple-hearted people, amongst other things I would have to give up the use of tobacco; and that, seeing that I had used it excessively for fifteen long years, was a terrible trial. I stopped at that point several days, not knowing what I should do. I really didn't believe I *could* give up using tobacco. It seemed as though it would be losing all there was worth living for in this world. I had repeatedly tried to part with it in years past, but the attempt had almost crazed me. I knew, or thought I knew, that if I made the attempt, the raging desire for the stimulant would beset me the moment I left the tent. Any of my readers who have used tobacco to excess know the full meaning of what I say.

And yet on the other hand I had longed for years to get forever rid of a habit that I felt to be disgusting, enervating and degrading. In the presence of a refined lady, I always remembered that I was liable to be detected in the use of the horrible weed. I was satisfied it was detrimental to health. I knew that tobacco-using robbed me of power as a temperance man. How many times it has come to me in the midst of a temperance address: How can you consistently urge these men to forsake one evil habit, liquor-drinking, while you are a slave to its twin-curse, tobacco.

All this, with the tremendous truth that he who uses tobacco defiles his body, which is the temple of the Holy Ghost, and thereby shuts himself out of spiritual light and willfully plods along in moral darkness, convinced my judgment that this was a vice to continue a moment longer in which would be sin. And yet came the response, How can I ever give it up? I now saw the point clearly: All genuine consecration is tested at *some* point, and, although there was not the slightest merit in my acceptance or rejection of the heavy cross as I regarded it, this point was where I was to meet with victory or defeat. At last I consented to go forword one evening amongst the seekers. Though somewhat dark, my mind needed but little instruction as regarded the way of salvation. I was determined to be a Christian. I had endeavored to count the whole cost. Still, here was the test question of giving up tobacco. As I knelt there a few of the friends gathered round, to whom, at last, I stated my position. They assured me that the very fact that God had convicted me so powerfully was proof that he wished to work out for me a great deliverance. I stated all my doubts and fears, when it was explained to me that Jesus was a perfect Saviour and would take away the *appetite* for tobacco or anything else that was sinful.

It seemed to me that I must give up. I could not bear to put off a matter of so much moment till a "more convenient season," and there was no possibility of crossing this spiritual Rubicon until the price was paid. Well, said I, at last, I shall try the experiment and test this matter to the bottom. By the help of God I have done with tobacco forever!

That was all. I had previously given up all else for Christ's sake, and I now took him for my blessed Saviour. The most I felt at the moment was a great, deep quietness of soul. Soon after I arose and retired. Near the door, all unseen, except by Him who was my helper, I drew forth a great roll of strong fine-cut tobacco, and threw it as far as possible into the tall grass. Since that hour I have never been troubled with the appetite for tobacco! My deliverance seems almost miraculous. Let every slave to this destructive drug, who really wants to get rid of his chains, take a similar course, and God will undoubtedly give him as glorious a victory. The scores of thrilling testimonies I have heard since that time, of a character similar to my own, are confirmatory of the truth of the statement which was made to me so confidently, and to which I adhere with all my heart: Faith in Christ will raise us above the power of any appetite.

I went straight home, and told my dear wife the step

I had taken, and there and then, at 3 o'clock in the morning, we re-erected the family altar which I had broken down so ruthlessly in the years of my cruel bondage. I trust, henceforth, its sacrificial fires will never go out. I always had an idea that my wife kept up family prayer, while I was a wanderer, which, I am glad to say, was really the case; but the husband ought to be the sacrificial priest of the household. I need hardly say how much my present decided act cheered the heart of the brave, patient woman who had prayed and hoped for this during so many weary years.

That evening I was conscious of no great outburst of feeling. I had finished my part of some great transaction. It was irrevocably done! and here I rested my case.

In the morning, early, it seemed as though a heavenly guest awakened me, and tenderly, lovingly, introduced me to a new life, wherein by faith I beheld Jesus as indeed my Saviour. Oh! what a flood of glory swept over my soul as I realized that "the past was under the blood;" that I was a Christian; that all the fearful wrong I had done stood against me no longer.

Since that time I can conscientiously say that I have been trying to walk in the light of God and do his whole will, and I thank his name for the blessings he has bestowed upon me and mine. My natural disposition is to be retiring and diffident; but, feeling called of God to the work, I have stepped into every Providential door to proclaim to the fallen and downtrodden ones of earth the Gospel of Temperance—the great, glorious truth that there is power in the blood of Jesus Christ to raise the poor drunkard, clothe him in his right mind, and send him forth a new creature. If, when the great Reckoning Day comes, it will be found that a few of the outcasts of society have been saved by such feeble instrumentality, how glad I shall be.

CHAPTER XIII.

ILLUSTRATIVE INCIDENTS.

The intelligent reader who has followed me thus far in my narrative, will have observed that I dwell with particular pains upon the statement of my belief that nothing short of the grace of God can enable a man to succeed in the work of reformation. I wish I could make this point as clear as its great importance would warrant. As one means to this end, I have thought that a few incidents selected at random from amongst those which have come under my own observation, bearing upon this branch of the subject, may prove interesting and profitable. Most of these cases came under my notice while I was a resident of the Washingtonian Home, Chicago, one of the best places in the world in which to study this subject. In mentioning certain cases I will adhere substantially to facts, although it will not be necessary to publish proper names, or even initials in some cases.

HARRY B. was a young man who, had it not been for the blight of strong drink, might have occupied a splendid position amongst his fellows. He was educated in the city of Montreal, Canada, and was a thorough linguist, speaking several languages fluently, and being thoroughly cultured in every other respect. A splendid penman, and skilled in almost every branch of business, he could command a good position almost anywhere. Unfortunately for himself, he learned amongst the young men of his native city to love the billiard-hall and to quaff, at last, the glass of wine-nectar. The young man who is governed by the high instincts of a gentleman and a man of the world, hides this species of wrong-doing from those he loves for a long time; but there comes a period when he feels that it will be impossible much longer to hide his excesses from loving eyes. Feeling this truth, Harry, with the blessing of his dear old mother on his head and followed by her prayers, departed for Chicago—to make for himself name and fortune in the great metropolis of the Northwest.—Fortune at once poured her favors at his feet. He was employed by one of the great firms of the city, and as his talents became known, he was speedily promoted, and in a very short time took his place as head book-keeper of the firm. What more could be desired? His salary would enable him to cultivate refined tastes, and if he would but take the right stand in society his career must necessarily be a bright and useful one.

But there was danger in the path. Harry was free-hearted, easy with his money, and in an evil moment he allowed himself to be led into the habits which had driven him from home. How easily they are acquired in a great city, and how difficult it is to get rid of them, is known to thousands of victims. The billiard-room was his besetment. It was easy to go out of its glare and glitter into deeper depths of vice, the doors of which were enticingly open at all times. For months this kind of life went on, and yet Harry contrived to appear each morning as though nothing was the matter, and to discharge his duties with fair ability. But, how true it is that Dissipation, as well as Murder, "will out." At last the employers of Harry B. learned that their head book-keeper was leading a life of dissipation. They were good men and could not bear the idea of turning him away for his sin; but they expostulated with him on his course, and besought him earnestly to reform. Poor Harry's proud spirit bent, and in his shame he promised he would have nothing more to do with the strong drink that lay at the bottom of all his troubles. In one week he had broken his vow and was in trouble deeper than ever. Then it went on from bad to worse, until the employers' patience became exhausted.

As a last resource, he entered the Home with a fixed determination to reform. His employers would not desert him while there was the least glimmer of hope. Morning and evening, for a length of time, they sent their private carriage to convey him to and from their place of business, lavishing upon him otherwise everything that kindness and esteem could suggest. He tried hard to reform—in his own way. He had his theories of reformation, as cold and heartless as the French philosophy he read, but Christianity must have no part in the work. On this point he was decided to the degree of stubbornness.

For many weeks he lived the quiet life of the Home, and his gentle behaviour and steady habits led all to hope that the work of reformation had taken deep root in his nature, and that he was going to win his way back to the position in society he had forfeited.

One Saturday night, however, he started down town. As that was not unusual with him, nothing was thought of it, until his non-appearance at bed-time created curious comment among the officers of the Home and those who had observed the correctness of his life for some months back. Morning came and with it no intelligence of Harry. Messengers were sent to the various police-stations, and still nothing could be heard as to his whereabouts.

Finally attention was directed to a paragraph in one of the Sunday-morning papers, describing the body of a young man killed during the night. The description seeming to indicate that the body was that of our missing companion, enquiry was made, and sure enough the awful discovery was made that the gifted Harry B. lay a mangled corpse.

On investigation, the facts of the case were discovered to be substantially as follows: On that fatal Saturday night, as he was passing the door of one of the flashiest billiard halls in the heart of the city, he stopped and remarked to an acquaintance that he owed the proprietor of the hall a small bill and would step in and pay. Suiting the action to the word he entered. The money being paid over, the proprietor, loth to lose such a fine customer, invited Harry to have a drink. At first he refused, but being urged, consented to drink something "very light." Then it was suggested that a game of billiards would be in order. Poor Harry had nothing but his own feeble will-power to help him stand up against this great temptation and it was but a few moments ere he was deeply absorbed in a game of billiards. The fatal step being taken, to order and imbibe drink after drink was a natural event.

A drunken man is apt to be hurried by the devil from one place to another. It was conjectured that Harry wandered in the dead hours of the night in search of some place or person until he stumbled into one of the great railway yards up-town, and, being confused with liquor, was thrown down by an engine and crushed out of all semblance of humanity. The mangled remains were brought home to us, but I will draw a veil over them. The sight was a terrible one.

Here was a young man, who felt his fall and degradation most keenly, and who longed to shake off the manacles that bound him. He had youth, and loving friends, and bright prospects to lure him on to virtue; he was surrounded by every consideration which could impel a man to true penitence and reformation—whether the awful death of those snatched away before our eyes by delirium tremens, or the example of those who proved by invoking and availing themselves of the power of One able to save. But he would be saved in his own proud way or not at all, and the young man of great promise and unbounded capabilities—the darling of a Christian mother—went down in this woful manner to the regions of darkness and despair.

THOMAS C. was a man of quite a different stamp: He was somewhat older and was a widower. He was a man, naturally, of sterling integrity of character, combining a clear intelligence with much acquired ability in his business; everybody liked him because his was a large, noble nature. He had always, however, discarded the claims of Christianity; even when his wife died, urging him to take a higher course. Instead of doing that which would have saved him, he tried to drown his deep sorrow in drink. Down, down he went in his rapid career until, as usual, all went into the mad vortex—character, home, business, health, happiness. He went to the Home in the desperate hope that he might be able to reform. Being a man of great will-power, he contrived by the aid of those who extended the helping hand, to regain his feet, and for many months no one could be found willing to cast any doubt upon the complete change that had taken place in the character of Thomas C. He held up his head once more amongst his fellows and seemed like a new man indeed. Still it was very clear that he held himself aloof from Christian influence, and seemed to scout the idea that it could have anything to do with a man's reformation from drinking habits. The man was trusting in his own strength—depending upon that force of character which is regarded with so much complacency as a man's chief reliance while in an unsaved state.

Our friend C. obtained a situation in the decorative department of one of the princely mercantile houses of the city, and for a time all went well. One day, however, some words of an angry nature with his employers led to his discharge.

With a man who was actuated by love to God, as an

active principle, this only meant a look around for a fresh situation, but it came with more force than Thomas C. had moral strength to bear.

A man who has once been addicted to drunkenness never forgets the power there is in alcohol to drown sensibility. That is one reason why so many thousands fly to drink the moment any calamity—real or fancied—comes upon them. So it was with the subject of this short sketch. He who had asserted (in his own strength) so frequently that he would *never* again touch the destroyer, in an unguarded moment, when passion swayed his soul, forgot his pledges and his former sorrows, and again sought solace in "drink."

What a sudden change took place: One night's orgie transformed the upright, gentlemanly mechanic into a filthy-looking creature who could only find proper associates in the vile whisky-saloon. To look at this trembling, tobacco-smeared, blaspheming creature, one could hardly by any stretch of the imagination, believe that it was the Thomas C. we had known the day before.

His downward career was very swift. High-strung men always descend rapidly—especially if they have been over the way before. In a week his best friend would barely recognize him, and where he may be to-day I will leave the reader to conjecture. I can only say, While there is life there is hope.

The above is another clear case of what is meant by the assertion that a man is in extreme danger, every day, of falling if all his efforts to stand up in the new life depend upon *self* as the sustaining power. Why, it is like erecting a fence of spider's web to check the onrush of a number of infuriated wild-beasts. Poor C. would not have Divine aid to help him, and he fell back into the horrible career of a drunkard.

McG. was a middle-aged Scotchman, and an oddity. One of those men whose character is made up of odd knobs, and kinks, and krinkles; who are hard to get hold of and harder still to handle. He was hard-headed, but somehow all his logic ran the wrong way. When sober he delighted in the arguments of Hume and the philosophy of George Coombe; under the influence of liquor he would preach the Gospel, while tears streamed down his cheeks. Poor Mc. was a very antithesis of humanity. While you agreed with him all was well; but cross him and take care, for you would hear the harsh Scottish twang, and feel a verbal arrow sticking in your ribs.

Our friend was a single man. At one time his warm Scottish nature had plunged him into a quagmire of intemperance, out of which he was pulled by some friends. He reformed, became a bright light in the temperance bodies—an oracle unto himself and everybody else. *He* not able to stand of his own strength of will, indeed! Why, was he not standing? Proof! away with the priestcraft idea that a man could not find all the elements of reformation from within.

This man stood four or five years, until at last he fell through a very simple cause: He had been for several years foreman of one of the departments of Pullman's Palace Car Works, and, in an evil moment, took his lunch in a neighboring restaurant where wine, beer, etc., composed a part of the bill of fare.

Afraid of the associations of such a place? Not he! He rather gloried in the opportunity of showing how strong he was. He knew what he was about, and if other people would mind their business, he was sure he had common sense enough not to make a fool of himself.

How it came about I never heard, precisely, but in a week or two McG. was picked up in the streets in a beastly state o" intoxication. The end came swiftly. The old appetite returned with tenfold fury; one excess followed another rapidly; the situation went, the decent clothing went; and in a few short weeks the devil had the proud, self-willed man dressed in his own livery. Where he is to-day I know not: but from his headlong nature I can see nothing before him, but the city hospital and a friendless grave.

The fate of W. W——, being that of a large class of young men, impressed us all very much. He was truly a representative Western young man. Tall, lithe, vigorous of frame. Intellectually he had very few superiors. His mind was of that regal kind which takes intelligence as an inherited right. He was at home in most branches of literature, while he was an adept in business. From the easy grace of his movements, the courtesy which marked his speech, and the gentlemanly behaviour that was manifested by him, one would be ready to say, There is a perfect character.

And yet, alas, there was a rankling evil within that fair exterior: W. loved alcoholic drinks. Periodically, like too many another good fellow, he found himself in their presence "weak as water." Oh! what mighty power that young man exerted, of his own accord, to stand against the overwhelming influence that was urging him to the brink of the precipice. It was insufficient—like the work of a child, with his wand, endeavoring to disperse an army.

Occasionly, it would seem that he had got the victory over appetite, but a week or two would dispel the illusion. There was little hope for him, because, despite the tears and entreaties of those who loved him, and the kindly efforts put forth to lead the poor sinner to the true remedy, he remained cold and obdurate as regarded the claims of Christianity. He could not and would not see why a man could not stand in the power that was his innately against strong drink. He wanted to be a reformed man, but he was not ready to be a Christian. It was easy to see, however, that each debauch brought him lower and lower. The end must be near—wha- kind of an end would it be?

One bright afternoon—I remember it well—W. entered his room, accompanied by a friend. They had both been drinking long and deep somewhere down in the city. The senses of poor W. were thoroughly confused. On his table stood a little bottle filled with aconite and labeled "Poison." The label was nothing to him just then, because the fluid looked like brandy. Seizing the bottle in his drunken frenzy, he uncorked it, and swallowed the contents.

In a few moments the quiet house was filled with the sound of agitated voices and hurried feet, and then two physicians and their assistants stood between the strong young man and Death. The struggle was an awful one;

but in one short half-hour all was over. Human skill had failed to overcome the deadly effects of the poison, and the one from whom we had a right to expect much had it not been for this curse, lay before us dead.

But why multiply these incidents? They are only a few amongst scores of a like character, all pointing to the same great truth. For a number of years, now, I have been investigating this s bject—seeking information wherever it can be found, and I am more thoroughly convinced to-day than ever, that if we trust to our own efforts to work out a complete reformation, failure will be the result.

I want to press this idea, in view of the noble fellows whom I have seen fall at my side in the battle of life, and of the bleaching bones of those whom I have known to fall out and die wretchedly by the way.

I am glad there is an opposite—and a glorious one to this dark side of the picture. There is a lit le army of men and women who, feeling their own power was weakness and except God saved they must perish, have made short work of reformation by calling upon the Lord for help.—In all these cases the work is instantaneous and thorough. No man who holds on to the arm of God to give him victory over strong-drink or any other object of appetite, can fail while that hold is retained. For evidence of the truthfulness of this assertion, I need only point to the evangelical churches of the land in which living witnesses are to be found—in greater numbers than ever before I am fain to believe. I had intended to mention a number of cases that came under my observation, but one or two will suffice.

Robert L. was another representative young man—from the hills of New Hampshire. Of splendid physique, he had a heart as tender as any woman's. Looking at the man and observing his nobility of character, one could not help asking over and over again, How came *he* ever to be a drunkard? That he did, however, was certain—not in the sense of the utmost degredation, but so clearly, in his own estimation, that he determined ere the disease became incurable to seek a permanent cure. Ere he could make up his mind as to the step he was prompted to take, he walked the streets of Chicago for a whole night.

In the morning he entered the Washingtonian Home. It was no light matter with him. He saw that he stood in a dangerous position, and while he had will-power enough left to make the start he was determined by the help of God to reform his life.

He was received gladly, and from the first hour of his residence in the institution, no one had the least doubt that he would be amongst those who would step out of the Home a free man. There was with him no sneer at religion and its claims—no argument as to the nature and effects of alcoholism. He knew the blighting effects of whisky-drinking and he went to work in the right way to apply the remedy. Wherever Robert went there seemed to be an atmosphere of Christian kindness. In the hospital, where Rum's finished work was to be found, the poor victims were soothed by his presence when all other means failed.

His employers did not look coldly upon him because he was an inmate of an inebriate asylum—thereby admitting that he needed reformation. Far from it. Much as they esteemed him before, this deliberate act seemed to endear him to them more closely than ever. Although the firm in which our friend held a responsible position, of a subordinate nature, was one of the heaviest, yet there was not a breath of suspicion that Robert would prove derelict to duty.

Did he succeed in reforming? Yes! of course. He commenced right, went right along, and left the institution beloved and honored by all. Behind him there remained an influence that rested sweetly upon many a heart. If I ever meet him in after life, I expect to grasp the hand of a man who has been rescued from a drunkard's loathsome career by Divine grace.

W. C. C. was a very hard case—deserted by friends, given up as lost by every grade of society in which he had lived, from the highest to the lowest. He was found one Sunday afternoon, in the Bridewell, or House of Correction, by a gentleman, who thought he could detect the glint of a diamond beneath all the filth and squalor. The gentleman actually spoke to him as though he had a soul beneath that miserable old coat—as if he thought all the man had not been stamped out of him. He drew out a sketch of his history, and learned that he had no hope of being a better man, simply because he had got too low for either God or man to care for him.

The practical Christian labored to convince the young man that he was cared for, and that if he made the necessary effort God would help him back to a sober life and *keep* him there.

A new light began to dawn upon C.'s mind. Perhaps it was possible for him to get rid of this accursed appetite—this degrading life of debauchery! If there was such a new, better life for him, he made up his mind that God helping him he would enter into it. He was taken into the Home, and very soon, in place of the ragged vagabond there appeared a MAN. What a transformation!

A few weeks afterwards, on the invitation being given for volunteer speakers in the "chapel" that young man arose, and in the eloquent tones true earnestness always gives, told the story of his life, and what a wonderful deliverance he had—ascribing the glory to God for his wonderful reformation.

He has stood the test of six years, and to-day he occupies as fine a position as any young man could wish for, honored by all who know him, an active member of an evangelical church, and a respected member of society.

Let these cases stand as representing the whole. It is a branch of the subject upon which I love to dwell; but this chapter has already swelled to too great a length.

CHAPTER XIV.

CONCLUSION.

Many hundreds, I hope, of my brethren in suffering, when they have read to this point will lay the book down and say, " Why, that is just my experience, in so far as the effects of drink are concerned! I have felt everything here described. Not a pang of misery, but I have felt the like; not one depth of degradation, but I have sounded; not a sigh ascended from this bruised heart, but there is one to respond to it from my bosom."

Well, my dear friends, I do not claim that my experience in suffering was more dreadful than that experienced by thousands of others, for it is all the same in quality. It makes my heart bleed sometimes to think of the thousands sitting in wretchedness and misery, who might be saved if some one could be found who cared enough for their souls to urge them for Christ's sake to fly for refuge to the only one who can save. Almost every time I address large audiences wives, and mothers, and sisters come to me with tears in their eyes, asking if something cannot be done for some erring, but still loved husband, son or brother. Ah, how little I can do after all to reach these poor sufferers. They are scattered far and wide. And yet I have thought a little volume like this might come to the wanderers as they sit in hopeless darkness, like a brotherly influence, to convince even *them* that there is a blessed hope of their restoration to society and the dear ones they have long since regarded as lost to them forever.

Experience and observation teach me that inebriates suffer more from utter Hopelessness than any other cause. They think there is no use trying to be better men: decent society has thrown them overboard; they have lost their business; everything looks dreary. How *can* they make a fresh start? I think I have answered that question in the preceding pages. O! my friend, make this effort in God's great name, and you will receive *exactly* the kind of help you want.

Take a strong stand for temperance. Dare to be a radical. Remember that the *pledge* that helps a man to permanent reformation is not one of man's devising, but is signed where only God is present, *away down in the depths of the soul.*

There is a false idea in existence that when a man is once down, he is down forever—that Society will frown him back to his darkness and his chains, no matter how great an effort he may make to recover himself. I want to disabuse the minds of my brethren on that point. If a man shows that he is in earnest, by taking off his coat and going to work as soon as he starts out in the new life; if he accepts the situation, determined that he will *die sober* if he can do no better, and holds fast to his integrity, depend upon it that struggling one will not want for a hearty grasp of the hand, or a cheery, "God bless you," as he pursues his upward way. I have watched this feature of the temperance question very closely, and I can honestly declare that the only time within five years I ever heard a reformed inebriate sneered at, was by the anonymous letter-writer of an Eastern weekly newspaper.

No! no! Society is only too glad to receive back, "Out of the Depths," the victims. It touches a chord in the great heart of Humanity too sacred and tender to admit of heaping reproach upon the head of the repentant one.

To many who would, perhaps, wish to reform, the objection may come : " I cannot avail myself of the aid of any public institution, what am I to do in that case?" I would say to such, Leave all that to the kind Providence which is enlisted in your behalf the moment you take the first decided step towards reform. No matter where you may be you will find friends to help you, and your efforts will be crowned with success.

As I look abroad in the temperance field and see men and women laboring in various ways to advance the good work, I can wish them success when these efforts bear the stamp of genuineness; but it is sometimes necessary to sift the tares from the wheat. All is not temperance that proclaims itself such. A great deal of mummery and nonsense needs to be cleared away from it, in my opinion. Many of the so-called "lecturers" are charlatans, pure and simple. Seeing that the subject has grown somewhat popular of late, they have floated to the surface, and endeavor by loud-mouthed declamation to make themselves heard.—These worthies depend upon a sort of high-toned sentimentality and an aptness for calling very bad names, but it can seldom deceive. The ring of the true metal is absent.

But there is no mistaking the true worker, whether in the prohibition field or the great moral movements which have been sweeping over the land for several years past. To all these my heart goes out in earnest well-wishes. As for myself, I am impelled, by the same Almighty Power that saved me to take my place by the fallen and broken-hearted. Let us all do our duty to the very utmost, looking for the reward hereafter.

It will doubtless be remarked by some that throughout this little volume I have not indulged in any very wild tirade against the liquor-sellers. Few, perhaps have more reason to do so; but, believing as I do, that such talk if indulged in promiscuously, does no good and wastes time, I have seldom done much in that direction. I would rather save one hard-working mechanic from a drunkard's grave than drive a hundred liquor-dealers wild with anger. Right well do I know that the low whisky-seller is after money, and cares not for body and soul if he can only secure *that*—that he will throw his victim out to die in the gutter, as soon as his last dollar has been spent; and yet my strongest feeling is to urge the working men of the land to give up drinking the accursed poison that is taking the clothes from the backs of their loved ones, and the manliness out of their own hearts.

Oh! my fellow-toilers, we have been keeping up the liquor-traffic. Let the hard-working men of the country cease consuming the substance of their families, and how long would it be ere those who depend upon their custom to obtain an easy living would be compelled to close their unsavory dens. Let me entreat you to throw aside the ensnaring cup. True, there are many in the world who can take liquor and leave it alone whenever they please, but only think how many thousands perish in attempting to discover whether or not they are among the number. I was to have been one of the number, but thanks be to God and His dear Son, Almighty Power that saved me to-day, I am not among the fallen and broken-hearted. Let us all do our duty to the very uttermost, looking for the reward hereafter.

Finally, it seems to me that I have come back from the very brink of a drunkard's awful hell to appeal to the Christian churches of the land, to see to it, that what they can do towards rescuing the fallen is done speedily and well. There is not a moment to lose. Many can be saved. Who are they? where are they? Let the church-members who are on fire with the Spirit of their Master visit some of the low places I have been describing, and they will find them—lifting up chained hands, and crying, "Who careth for my soul?" The churches have done a glorious work within the past few years; and yet it is only commencing. See how much yet remains unharvested! Reapers! Reapers!

THE END.

The Temperance Book for the Times.

OUT OF THE DEPTHS;

A

PERSONAL NARRATIVE

OF

My Fall Under the Power of Strong Drink

AND MY

COMPLETE REFORMATION.

BY W. T. COX.

"Out of the Depths have I cried unto Thee, O Lord."—Psa. cxxx. 1.

SYCAMORE, ILL.
BAKER & ARNOLD.
1876.

Pointed, Truthful, Heart-stirring.

PRICE—25 CENTS PER COPY—*Agents Wanted.*

www.ingramcontent.com/pod-product-compliance
Lightning Source LLC
Chambersburg PA
CBHW020326090426
42735CB00009B/1416